Knot Tying

How to Tie Basic Rope Knots for Outdoors

(Untie All Manner of Everyday Knots in Different Styles)

Dionne Espino

Published By **Jorden levy**

Dionne Espino

All Rights Reserved

Knot Tying: How to Tie Basic Rope Knots for Outdoors (Untie All Manner of Everyday Knots in Different Styles)

ISBN 978-1-7780579-2-2

No part of this guidebook shall be reproduced in any form without permission in writing from the publisher except in the case of brief quotations embodied in critical articles or reviews.

Legal & Disclaimer

The information contained in this ebook is not designed to replace or take the place of any form of medicine or professional medical advice. The information in this ebook has been provided for educational & entertainment purposes only.

The information contained in this book has been compiled from sources deemed reliable, and it is accurate to the best of the Author's knowledge; however, the Author cannot guarantee its accuracy and validity and cannot be held liable for any errors or omissions. Changes are periodically made to this book. You must consult your doctor or get professional medical advice before using any of the suggested remedies, techniques, or information in this book.

Upon using the information contained in this book, you agree to hold harmless the Author from and against any damages, costs, and expenses, including any legal fees potentially resulting from the application of any of the information provided by this guide. This disclaimer applies to any damages or injury caused by the use and application, whether directly or indirectly, of any advice or information presented, whether for breach of contract, tort, negligence, personal injury, criminal intent, or under any other cause of action.

You agree to accept all risks of using the information presented inside this book. You need to consult a professional medical practitioner in order to ensure you are both able and healthy enough to participate in this program.

Table of Contents

Chapter 1 – What is Knot Tying? 1

Chapter 2: What to Do When In a Survival Situation 5

Chapter 3: Times When You Need Survival Knots 9

Chapter 4: Some of the Broad Knot Categories 17

Chapter 5: Other Handy Knot Categories 24

Chapter 6: Surviving the Wilderness the Knotty Way 30

Chapter 7: Climbing Knots 46

Chapter 8: Survival Knots 61

Chapter 9: Knot Tying 101 87

Chapter 10: Basic Knots 99

Chapter 11: Knots For Campers 112

Chapter 12: Knots For Sailors & Fishermen . 131

Chapter 13: Knots For Rock Climbers & Mountaineers 157

Chapter 14: Knots For Farms & Animals........ 178

Conclusion.. 183

Chapter 1 – What is Knot Tying?

Knots are made from the tying or fastening of ropes and cords which is commonly useful and sometimes used for decorative purposes. Knot tying is a practice of bending two rope ends or cord ends by bringing them together and performing different loops that varies on the worker's desire.

The practice of knot tying takes a lot of time, but if you're willing to invest in it, you can be a professional in no time. There are different types of knots that have its own purpose, because first of all not all knots works in the same manner or application. We'll be listing down these kinds of knots:

- Bend- ever wonder what are the knots used for climbing ropes. These knots are what we called bend knots, it is formed by uniting the two ends of the rope or cord of the same line. There are also different types of bend knots:

Adjustable Bend- this is the most common one, it is a kind of bend that can be easily adjusted for lengthening or shortening.

- Beer Knot- this is the specific bend applied in constructing slings used in rock climbing as it holds very tight.

- Ashley's Bend- it is a knot used in securing the ends of two ropes together. Like the other common types of knots, it also features two interlocking overhand knots.

- Butterfly Bend- it is the knot used in joining the two ends of two ropes together.

- Albright's Special- it is a bend used for angling, known for its strength, it used to join two different diameters of line.

- Blood knot- this knot is the most useful knot when you're fishing.

- Carrick Bend- this is the bend that is commonly used for very heavy ropes or cords that is too large.

- Harness Bend- it is a bend that can be pulled before securing.

Binding- it is a knot used to keep two objects together.

- Coil Knot- these are the knots used to keep ropes and cables together.

- Decorative Knot- these are the knots used in decorative purposes, they're commonly made of repetitive patterns of knots or in different shapes.

- Hitch- a knot that is tied usually on cables and rings.

- Lashing- a type of knot that is used to hold poles.

- Loop- used to create a circle in a line.

- Plait- sometimes called braid, is made from a single simple line pattern.

- Slip- it is the loops contrast, as you pull the loop it can be closed but the slip knot can't be.

- Slipped- one great example of a slipped knot is the tying of your shoelace.

- Seizing- it is a knot used for holding two lines together.

- Sennit- unlike the plait that has only a simple pattern, this knot has a complex one.

- Splice- takes time to make but the strongest type of knot.

- Stopper- a knot you can see that holds the line inside a hole.

- Whipping- it binds the rope or cord to prevent a line from fraying.

Although some of these knots are difficult to practice, it is worth knowing that they can be useful in certain scenarios. Sometimes, these knots may save your life, especially when you're lost in the forest or other survival scenarios that you can use these knots.

Chapter 2: What to Do When In a Survival Situation

Maybe call mum... or maybe dad... or your dear friend who isn't on this trip with you. Or probably that can wait as you check out what you can bite before long – you can enjoy a meal as you think. Well, none of these options sounds like the best for starters, in cases where you can see the dangerous potential of remaining stranded for an indefinite period of time. How did this even happen, anyway? The fact is that you cannot sort anything out in any helpful manner if you fall into panic mode.

First Things First When You Are Stranded

(1)Halt

You need to relax if you are to think straight and logically. That is why the first step needs to be you stopping everything – not walking forwards, not moving backwards; just stopping. By so doing, you are giving yourself time to cool down your frustration, to dissipate your anger, and calm your nerves, which, very likely, will have been on edge due to fear.

(2)Weigh your options

After you are reasonably calm, you can now begin to evaluate your situation. Remember even before you know if you are going to build a shelter, a boat or anything else, your most important survival tool is your good brain. In such circumstances, every brain must be great – no choice.

(3)Begin observing your surroundings

As you are observing your surroundings, make a point of taking in all the pertinent challenges that the area presents, and also the pertinent advantages it may present. For example, if you notice a winding path in the bushes, you will have an idea that some people sometimes venture into the area and might be of help to you. At the same time, it may be indication that anyone searching for you, just in case someone has an idea where you went out to, is likely to use the path. You may, therefore, decide to stick around instead of moving to another location.

(4) It is now time to plan your cause of action

Needless to say, planning comes with prioritization. For instance, unless you are stranded in a place with network and your phone is in operation and so you can use the pictures to attract help, it would not make much survival sense to begin taking photographs. Much as photographs make for good memories, you may wish to prioritize the issue of food and shelter.

In fact, do not fumble with how to prioritize. Experts recommend:

- Handling the shelter issue first, especially because you need to protect yourself from the harsh weather elements
- Building a fire to keep you warm
- Designing the best signal you can to try and attract attention
- Searching for a water source

That issue of building a shelter is actually one of the major reasons you need to learn to tie different kinds of knots. A shelter becomes your base when you are stranded in the wilderness, and even when you go out searching for food and scouting the area for any sign of human intervention, you still look forward to getting back to your shelter.

Needless to say, your movements may not necessarily be easy, and sometimes you may wish to have access to high areas; places that call for your climbing skills. If you are equipped with knot tying skills, you may manage to build tools to help you to climb up to the vantage points you are seeking. Knot tying skills also come in handy when you find a natural water source where you think you might find fish for food. In fact, you may even wish to build snares, to see if you might catch some small animal that you can convert into meals – animals such as hares and wild duck.

Chapter 3: Times When You Need Survival Knots

What would we say survival knots, really are? Well, as for survival knots, there is no ambiguity. There are two key words here – knots and survival. The reason you want to learn how to make knots is so that they can get you out of trouble when you are stranded and all you are hoping for is to be able to get out in one piece. What kind of trouble could you, possibly, be in, to require the use of knots? Patience please… We are coming to that soon. In the meantime, what are knots themselves? A knot is exactly what the dictionary says it is – a fastening that you make by tying a piece of cord; a string; a rope; or something else that you can twist and tie.

A knot is not something strange, really, if you consider that people are tying their ties every day. Tying a tie is actually making a knot using a tie. However, the kinds of knots this guide is focusing on are unique in that you need to make every single one of them to suit the need at hand. If you are not skilled you might find yourself jumping from the frying pan to the fire. For instance, you may need to get out of a burning storey building fast, and all you have are several pairs of sheets that you could tie together and use to lower yourself down through a window. Do you see how it matters in this case the type of knot you make? You need to tie the sheets together using the appropriate knots, because using the wrong knots could see your sheets sliding apart and putting your life at risk.

The chapters that follow will focus on the types of knots that you may need to use when stranded in remote areas, like the places scouts often go on trips, or where disciplined forces like the army venture in the course of duty. And with this statement, you can already visualize the kind of trouble you might fall into, to call for the use of knots. You will soon see the various uses different knots are put to, and how they end up helping people to survive in the wilderness. Some challenges that may require you to employ your knot tying skills include:

- Securing tarpaulins to make shelter

- Using barks of trees to tie branches when making shelter
- fastening guy lines on things like tents
- tying lines for use in hanging lanterns
- tying wires and other material to build snares

What do these challenges reveal? Well, they point to the fact that you need to tie knots when you are stranded away from civilization and needing to build a make-shift shelter. Not only would you require protective cover over your head to shield you from weather elements like rain, ice and extreme sunshine, you would also need food. That's the reason one challenge mentioned above is that of making snares. Once you are stranded in the wilderness, you may need to catch wild rabbit and such other animals to make meals out of them. Being able to build a shelter with the local material available and to make a meal with the resources available in the wilderness, can make the difference between surviving long enough to be rescued, or long enough to find your way out, and literally dying in the woods.

Is it really possible to envisage all situations where you may need to tie something to help in your survival in remote places? No, it isn't really possible to do this, and that is the reason it is important that you read a guide as informative and as simplified as this one, so that if it happens that you are in a fix away from civilization, you wouldn't panic, and your life would not be endangered.

Relevant Terminologies

Can you effectively explain matters relating to tying a tie without mentioning a shirt? Obviously, no, because the tie you are tying is, ultimately, going to hang around the collar of your shirt. Likewise, knots must go with ropes or such other similar items such as strings. In fact, it is the rope itself that you use to practice tying the kind of knot you have in mind. Needless to say, if you are seeking to survive in a wild place, you cannot depend on weak items like strings to fulfill many of your major requirements, such as securing a tarpaulin. As such, this chapter will explain in simple terms the meaning of some terminologies that are specific to tying knots. Once you understand their meaning, it will be relatively easy for you to appreciate the explanation provided regarding tying a knot.

Terminologies Used In Tying Various Knots

(1) Wraps

You make a wrap when you take your rope winding around two poles or two sticks, or even when you take the rope winding around three poles or three sticks. When only two poles or sticks are involved, you will hear the term, *square lashing,* being drawn into the usage. And when three poles or sticks are involved, you will hear the term, *tripod lashing,* being drawn in as well.

At the beginning of every wrap is a clove hitch, meaning there is a knot being used on the rope, where you pass the rope two times around another rope sometimes, and other times around a spar. Whether you use a spar or another rope, the original rope crosses it at a right angle. As for spar, think of it as a strong pole, one presumed to be thick, like the one you find used as a ship mast. The wraps and the clove hitches are part of what forms a lashing – especially when getting tightened with fraps.

(2)Fraps

Fraps are means by which you tighten your lashings, looping your rope around the wraps in a perpendicular manner; all meant to hold your spars, or the sticks you are using, together.

(3)Lashings

Lashings are what you form when you engage your wraps as well as fraps in tying two or, maybe, three spars or even sticks, together to create solid corners. Alternatively, you carry out the same exercise, but this time to build tripods. At each end of a lashing is a clove hitch.

(4)Lay

This simply refers to the twist you make with the rope

(5)Loop

This is actually an opening that you create from doubling over a rope or something like that. In our context, look at it as crossing the rope's running end either over or under the rope's standing end, so that ultimately it forms a circle or a ring.

(6) Pig tail

If you visualize a knot tying incident, every time you do it, isn't there some part of rope left loose after all is done? That is the part referred to as pig tail, and it is supposed to be a maximum of 4" or around 10cm, otherwise you may cause unnecessary interference in whatever you are trying to do with your rope. At the same time, you don't want the pig tail to become a waste of precious rope at this time when you are in your dire situation.

(7) Running end

Take this to be that part of your rope which you are holding and twisting with a view to tying your chosen type of knot.

(8) Standing end

This happens to be that part of the rope that you are not actively using; the part that is static. In fact, take the whole of your rope besides the running end to be the standing end.

(9) Turn

When you make a loop around, say, a rail or any other object, and your rope's running end happens to be proceeding away from the standing end, meaning that the standing end and the running end are moving in opposite directions, the loop you have just made is the one referred to as the turn.

(10) Round turn

This is when the continuing part of the running end makes a circle and then exits in the direction of the standing end.

(11) Whipping

The action you take, however you do it, in order to prevent your rope end from unwinding or untwisting. Often you do it by wrapping the rope end very tightly using a tiny cord. Other times you hold it tight with tape or such like item with adhesion.

When do you do the whipping? Ideally, you need to do the whipping before you make a cut at the spot where you want to divide the rope into two. The reason for this timing is to prevent the cut rope from untwisting right there.

Chapter 4: Some of the Broad Knot Categories

If you are a sailor, you probably know some of these knots, and if you are a scout or a girl guide, you may be familiar with a number of them too. This is because you have probably spent hours or nights out, not as part of your plan, but because you have been inconvenienced by some of your basic structures working. While guides and scouts may have concerns about strengthening their tarpaulins and tents to protect them against strong winds, sailors might be worried that some ship mast could be blown off and leave them stranded with their vessel at sea.

Still, knowledge about tying different types of knots may come in handy for you even when you are neither a scout or guide, nor a sailor, especially considering how much travel there is today. Or don't you think you could travel long distance by car and your car breaks down in the middle of nowhere? Depending on the location you are stranded in, you might find it safer to set camp in the forest close by, rather than sit down or stand by the roadside attempting to hitchhike.

All the same, is it not enough to learn one or two types of knots? No, it isn't. There are some ropes and cords that will only hold tight with specific knots, sometimes depending on the material they are made of; other times owing to their texture; and so on. At the same time, some situations call for certain types of knots while the same knots may be entirely inappropriate for other situations. In short, you are better off the more knots you know how to tie. This chapter is going to explain various knots and categorize them according to the need they fulfill.

Stopper; End of line; and Midline Knots

1. Stopper knots

The reason you want stopper knots is that you have something you want to stop from sliding or from moving from its position. Examples of stopper knots include the Figure 8 knot; the overhand knot; the double overhand knot; the *Stevedore* knot; and also the *Ashley Stopper Knot*. Of all these stopper knots, Figure 8 is the more sought after. However, the Estar knot is most recommended if your rope is slippery.

The Figure 8 Knot

This knot is also referred to as the Flemish knot. In case you want to do some climbing, the Figure 8 comes in very handy.

Here is an image of it:

How to tie the Figure 8:

What you do is pick the tail of the rope and use it to form a loop. Once you have your loop, continue taking the rope underneath and then around the rope's standing end. To complete tying your Figure 8 knot, now pass the tail down through the loop you made.

This knot mainly serves as a stopper knot. Whatever you are trying to hold with the rope remains well secured because of this knot. Apart from the role the Figure 8 plays in securing something in position, it is also convenient to untie it. However, this advantage could be a weakness in some situations, because sometimes the knot can slip loose without you noticing and you would have to tie it again.

2. End of Line knots

This is the knot you tie right at the end of your rope so that it forms a loop or something like it, for the purpose of attaching the object you want to anchor, or the thing you want connected to the rope. The double bowline knot seems to be the most popular.

Image of the Double Bowline Knot

3. The midline knots

If your rope has been damaged some place, it is the midline knot that you tie in order to render the damaged part of your rope redundant. How you do that is by forming a loop so that you clip that damaged section or you entirely bypass it. A good example of the midline knot is the butterfly knot, which also goes by the name, lineman's rider or lineman's loop.

As for tying it, you can form the butterfly knot without making use of either end of the rope. This attribute makes this knot very convenient when the rope being used is very long. In a climbing attempt, for instance, the butterfly knot comes in very handy.

The Butterfly Knot Image

4. Knots joining two ropes, sometimes with varying diameters

A good example of this type of knot is the double fisherman's rod.

Double Fisherman's Rod Image

Chapter 5: Other Handy Knot Categories

Safety; Hitch; and Tied loop Knots

Hopefully, by now you are able to see the importance of having skills to tie knots in different ways. The type of knot that would keep a climber safe when scaling a high wall to safety, is not, necessarily the one that would suit someone trying to erect a shelter using tree branches and a tarpaulin. This chapter is going to introduce other broad categories of survival knots, also classified according to the need they fulfill.

Incidentally, do you recall what the different parts of a knot are? It is very important to keep them in mind so that every time you read about the part to hold, you are clear about where to correctly touch.

- When you talk of the line you mean the rope that you are using

- As for the working end, you recall is the part you actively hold and twist in the process of tying your knot

- The standing part being that one which is lying idle during the process of tying the knot; when you are technically doing the rigging

- And when your rope takes a U-turn you call that a bight of rope

Here are more broad categories of survival knots

1. Safety knots

Have you tied your knot, whatever category it falls under? Now what you need to follow up with in order to keep that knot you've made secure, is to make another knot. We are looking at a scenario where your original knot might begin unraveling. This second knot that is meant to protect your original knot from deforming comes right at the tail of your rope. A barrel knot is a good example of a safety knot.

<u>The Barrel Knot</u>

You shouldn't be surprised to see it being referred to as the *blood knot*. This survival knot comes in very handy especially when you are using a cord that could easily lose its inherent strength after being twisted to make a knot. Think of a monofilament nylon line, for example.

The way to go about tying a barrel knot is making your two lines overlap for a distance of around 6cm – 8cm. In the meantime, you ensure that the short end of those two lines face opposite directions. After that you need to pick the short end of your line and wrap it four to six times well around your second line. Now bring the remaining section of the first short end back and ensure it passes in between your lines where the wraps begin. The second line's short end will now need to be wrapped four to six times around your first line. At the same time, you'll be bringing back the end of your first line, and passing it through the oval shaped space you'll have created right between the initial wrap of each of the sets you'll have made.

The Barrel Knot Image

2. The Hitch

As for the hitch, you need to think about a knot that you tie around an object, and that knot assumes the shape of that object. What this essentially means is that the minute you remove that object around which your knot is made, the knot loses its shape. A good example of the hitch is the Prusik hitch, which is sometimes referred to as the friction hitch.

As for use, you'll mostly find it used in mountaineering; rope rescue missions, and such other undertakings.

The Prusik Hitch Image

3. Tied Loop

When you make this knot, what you see is something that looks like a fixed eye at the end of your rope. It's actually a kind of loop. A good example of a tied loop is the bowline knot. Many users acknowledge the ease with which you tie a bowline knot, and also the ease with which you untie it when you want to. Even when there is the impact of a load, you still find it easy to undo the bowline knot. This knot is so important especially in the maritime world that it is referred to as the *King of Knots.*

The Bowling Knot Image

Chapter 6: Surviving the Wilderness the Knotty Way

After calming your nerves and coming up with a plan on how to handle your situation in the wilderness, your plan is likely to be challenged, sometimes because the location you find yourself in happens to have wild animals, or the equipment you have simply do not work well. For instance, you may have a tent in your possession, but it got messed up somewhere and cannot stand steady. You may also need to spend your night for your own security. What are you going to do if the trees are tall, slippery, and without much grip?

Using the Taut line Hitch to Steady Your Tent

The Taut line Hitch

You can use a taut line hitch to strengthen your tent protecting it from being blown off by strong winds.

What, exactly, is a taut line hitch and how does it work?

The taut line hitch is an adjustable hitch, which you tie on that standing part after securing it around the object at hand. To tie a taut line hitch, all you need to do is slip the knot in a way that it tightens the line, holding it fast under the weight. What you actually end up with is a loop knot that is easy to adjust at will. It is a knot that is very useful when lines require adjusting, either in a bid to loosen them or to tighten them. You may sometimes hear the taut line hitch being referred to as the *rigger's hitch*; the *midshpman's hitch*; the *tent hitch*; or even the *tent line hitch*.

Ordinarily when you find yourself tying the knot around another object besides the taut line's own standing part, you are going to speak of it as a rolling hitch. Also, when the knot tying is such that the 2nd turn is somewhere between the 1st turn and the standing part, the term adopted is the midshipman's hitch.

This taut line hitch is a knot that is very popular with campers, as they are great for securing tent guy lines. The reason it works so well on tents is that it slides freely, and it is still capable of jamming under the load, making it easy to adjust the line as necessary. When *Boy Scouts of America* speaks of the recommended adjustable sliding knot, the taut line hitch is what they are referring to. The important point to take away from here is that if ever you want to make adjustments to the way your tent is holding in the wilderness, and especially if your tent has been destabilized by winds or other weather elements, the taut line hitch is the best knot to employ.

How to tie a Taut line Hitch

- Begin by turning your line around a post or whatever object you are using, ensuring the place you are tying the knot is many feet away from the free end

- Now pick the free end and coil it twice around that part that is the standing line, as you work backwards in the direction of the post

- Next, do some other coiling once around your standing line, and that needs to be outside the coils you've already made

- You can now tighten your knot, sliding it on your standing line in order to adjust the tension.

    Some people simply describe the taut line hitch as two ½ hitches that have an additional turn.

    <u>The Taut line Hitch Image</u>

Other Sensitive Uses of the Taut line Hitch

- If you find yourself in the wilderness with an aircraft that requires tying down.

- If you need to climb up trees that are not easy to tackle, probably to keep yourself safe or to have a better view of the horizon

- If you want to evacuate from the area and you want to secure loads on whatever carrier you have

Chapter 2 – Knot Tying Projects For Sewing

Sewing is also common these days, but people tend to sew automatically nowadays because, for some, manual sewing can take a lot of time and effort. But enough of the automated ones, today we'll tackle about the different knot tying used for sewing, from common ones to the ones you probably didn't hear about.

Starting with the first project. The standard knot in sewing, it is the common way on how to hold the sewing thread into the needle. Some may find it hard doing this especially on the part of inserting the sewing thread into the needle's eye but in reality, the steps are pretty easy. Here they are:

-

☐   Step 1: Hold the sewing thread with your two fingers, it depends on what hand you'll be using, if you're right or left handed, it is not a big deal. These steps will still apply perfectly.

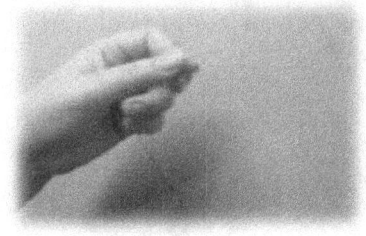

☐   Step 2: Bring the sewing thread closer to your two fingers, as having a very long allowance of the thread will make it hard for you to insert it inside the needle. After insert it inside the needle, you might want to wiggle it around so that it will fit perfectly on the hole.

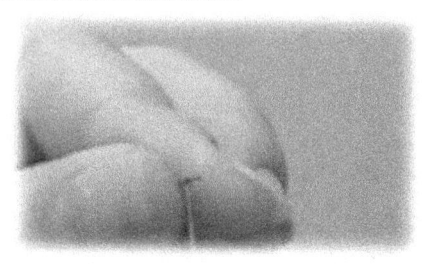

☐ Step 3: When already inserted, pull through until you get in the middle of the sewing thread, when the needle is already there, get the two end lines of the sewing thread and

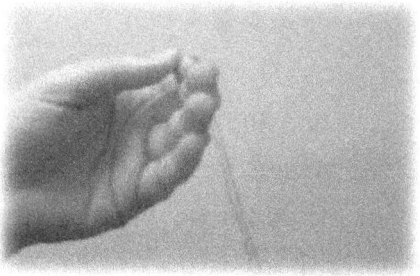

hold them with your forefinger and thumb.

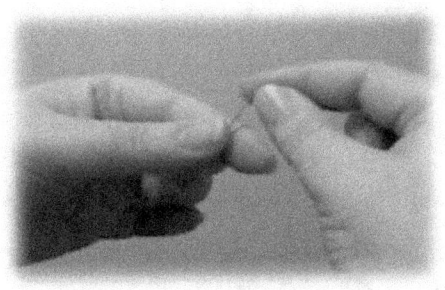

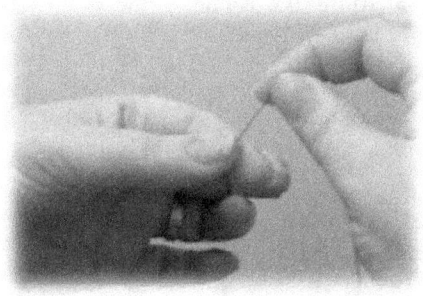

☐   Step 4: While holding on the two ends of the sewing thread, start wrapping it up on your forefinger to create a loop. You'll see an 'x', don't put too much allowance on the end line, and just make it short.

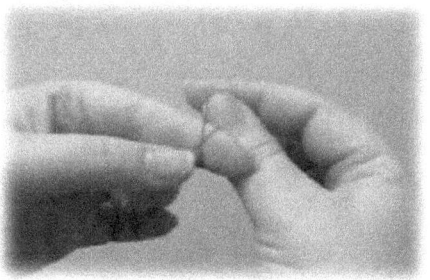

☐   Step 5: Hold on to the middle of the 'x' then start rubbing it while pulling slowly away from your forefinger, in this way the end line and the main loop will join temporarily.

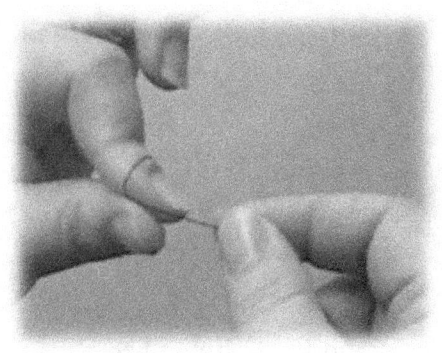

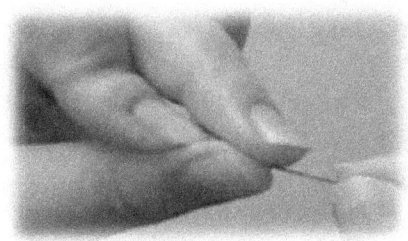

☐ Step 6: When the loop reaches the end of your finger, grab the end line of the loop than start pulling it to make the knot.

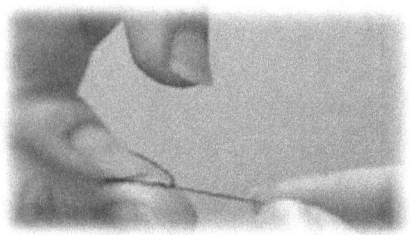

☐ Step 7: The knot should like this, and then bring the needle back to that know created after that you're good to go.

Finishing knot on the back stitch- this step-by-step tutorial will show you on how to properly finish the ending stitch at the back of your fabric or cloth you've been sewing. Pay close attention.

☐ Step 1: The front stitch facing you, take the last stitch and push it through the other side using the needle.

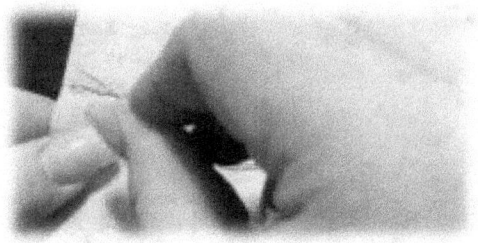

☐ Step 2: Now flip over the fabric, then you can see the pushed side of the end stitch at the front.

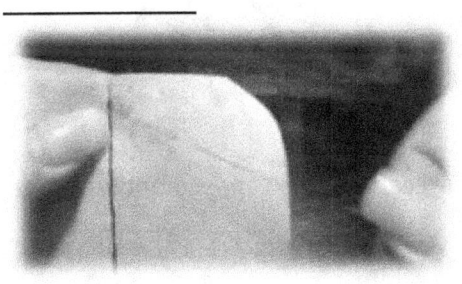

☐ Step 3: Insert the needle on that hole created by the pushed end of the stitch at the front.

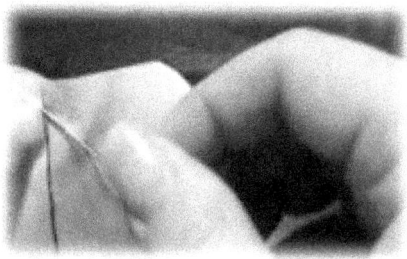

☐ Step 4: When the needle is inserted, stop at the middle. Do not insert it fully.

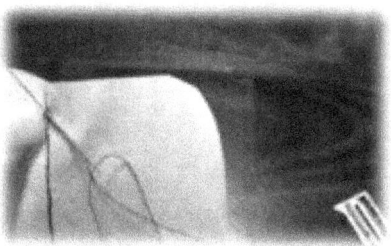

☐ Step 5: You can see two thread endings, one inside the needle and one in the fabric. Grab the one in the fabric.

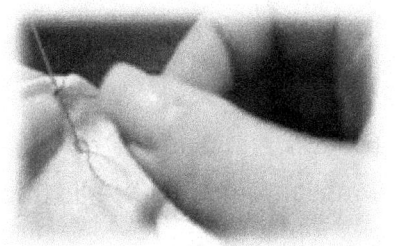

☐ Step 6: After grabbing the end stitch of the fabric, wrap it around the needle three times.

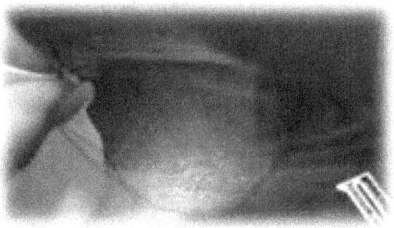

☐ Step 7: Then, after making the three wraps around the needle, push it downward and hold it with your thumb and forefinger tightly.

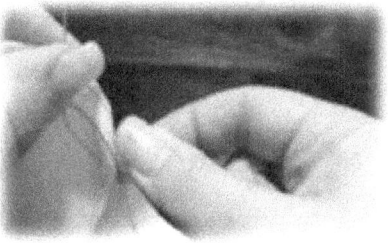

☐ Step 8: Then start pulling the needle upwards with your other hand while the other one is holding tightly on the three wraps you made.

☐ Step 9: After pulling it upwards, the knot must now appear, then for the final step, cut off the excess thread. Now you have your clean back stitch with a knot.

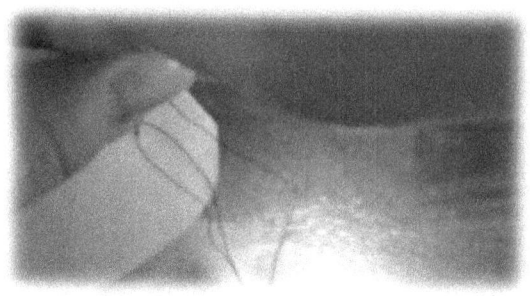

Chapter 7: Climbing Knots

In this chapter, you will learn how to tie some basic climbing knots such as Bowline, Figure 8, Double Fisherman's Bend, Clove Hitch, Alpine Butterfly Loop, and Munter Hitch. As these are climbing knots, you will use ropes for tying them.

The most famous and versatile climbing knot is probably the Bowline. This is a knot you can trust. If, for instance, you are climbing and you want to tie yourself and make sure you won't slip, this is the knot to use. It will easily come untied after use no matter how much weight is put on it.

CAUTION:

Whenever climbing ropes are used there is a risk of danger. Take proper precautions to make sure everyone stays safe.

Bowline

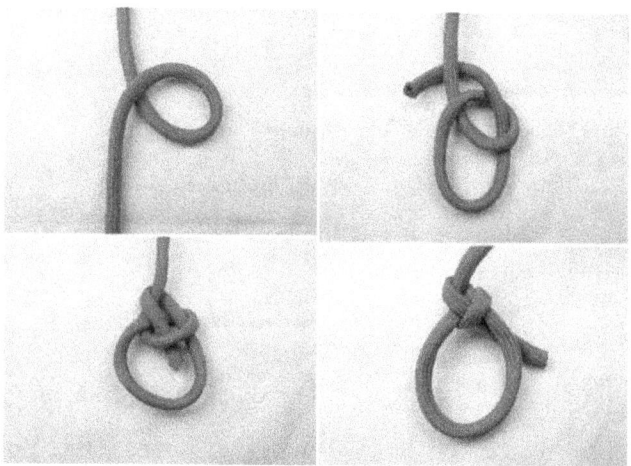

Method:

Step 1: Take a rope and make a loop at the left side of the line.

Step 2: Take the right end of the line, go underneath the loop and then through the loop.

Step 3: After that, go around the other side of the rope (the left side where you made the first loop) and then back through the whole.

Step 4: Pull the other side of the rope up, and you just make the bowline knot.

Figure 8 Follow Through Loop

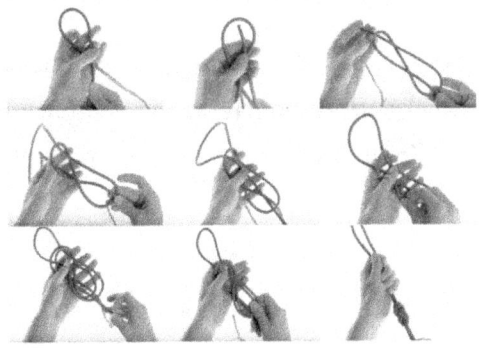

Method:

Step 1: First tie a loose figure 8. To do that, make a loop and then bring the tail under the rope and through the loop.

Step 2: Then, follow the original figure 8 with the tail and exit the knot to create the follow through figure 8.

Step 3: Tighten the knot so that the outside loops tighten next to the adjoining turns.

Step 4: For the stopper, wrap the tail once, then cross over the wrap and feed the tail back down under both loops to create the stopped knot.

Figure 8 Loop On A Bight

Note: This is essentially a standard figure 8 but instead of bight is passed through the loops instead of a tail.

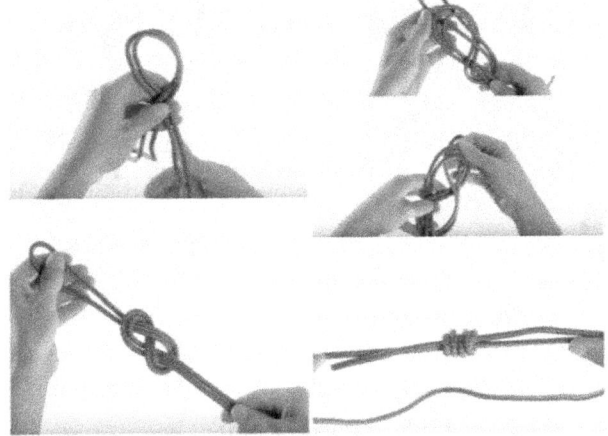

Method:
Step 1: Take a large bight and create a loop.

Step 2: Pass the bight under the rope and back up through the loop.

Step 3: Tighten down in the same fashion as the previous figure 8.

Double Fisherman's Bend

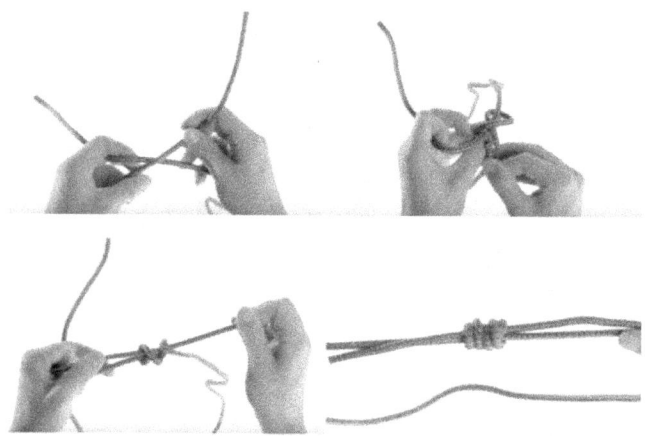

Method:

Step 1: Overlap the two ends and wrap one end around both ropes two full turns.

Step 2: Pass the end back through the turns and pull it tight.

Step 3: Next, pass the other end two full turns around both ropes and pass the tail through.

Step 4: Pull both ropes to tighten the two ends against each other.

Clove Hitch

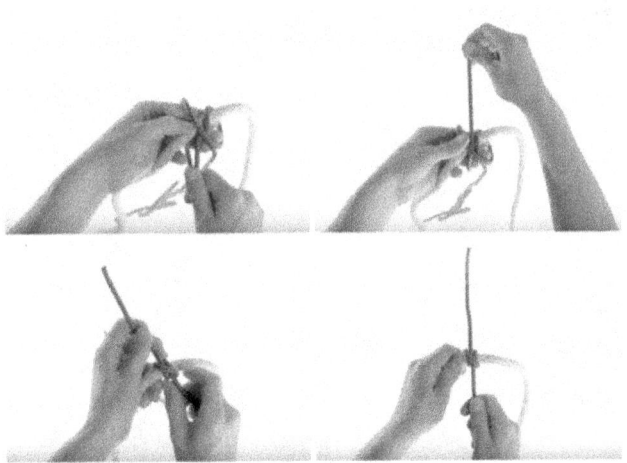

Method:

Step 1: To start a clove hitch, pass the end of the rope around the anchor point.

Step 2: Continue over the standing end and around a second time.

Step 3: Thread the end under these loops and pull tight.

Alpine Butterfly Loop

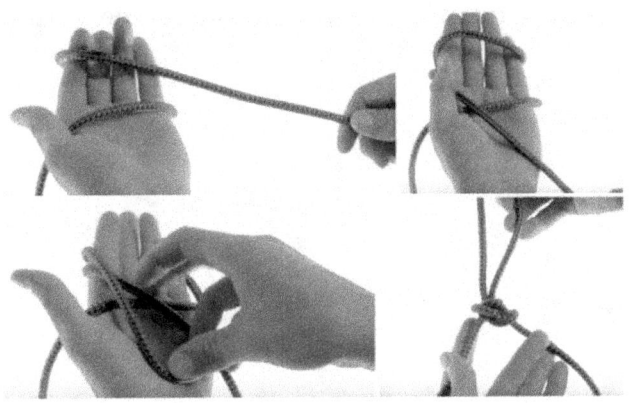

Method:

Step 1: Wrap the rope around your hand twice.

Step 2: At the end of the first wrap, make sure the rope is close to your fingertips. Continue around a finish the second near your thumb.

Step 3: Pick up the turn near your fingertips and wrap it around the other two, then slide the knot off your hand.

Step 4: Tighten by pulling both ends of the rope.

Munter Hitch

Method:

Step 1: Pass the tail through the carabiner.

Step 2: Then make a loop and pass that through the gate.

Step 3: Tighten down the munter on the carabiner. The munter is now set for descent.

Step 4: For ascent, reverse the ropes and the knot is pulled through the carabiner.

Munter Hitch With Mule Hitch Stopper

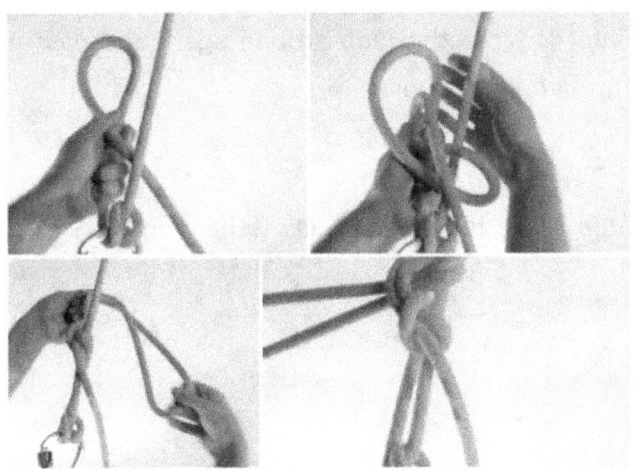

Method:

Step 1: To tie the munter off with a mule hitch stopper, create a loop on one side.

Step 2: Then, pull the tail under the rope.

Step 3: Pass a second loop over and through the first and then tighten down.

Step 4: Wrap the loop around again and pass it through that opening.

Step 5: Tighten down to tie off the munter.

Chapter 8: Survival Knots

You will use these survival knots while you are doing some outdoor activities such as camping. As with climbing knots, you will use ropes to ties these knots.

The knots that may be useful and that you will learn how to tie in this chapter are the Timber Hitch, Trucker Hitch, Cat's Paw, and Taut-Line Hitch. Let's see what these knots are used for.

The Timber Hitch is one of the knots that you can use to make a tarp shelter quickly, as it serves as one of the anchor points for your shelter. The knot is easy to untie.

The Trucker Hitch is another knot that you can use to pitch a tent. It is used to cinch down your main line and make it really tight.

There is another version of this knot and it can be used when you need to something say like on top of your car and tighten it down quite a lot.

Cat's paw knot is a knot commonly used to attach a cord or rope to objects and it comes in a single, double or triple version.

Taut-line hitch is a knot you can use if you want to pitch a tent and you wanto tie a rope between tow objects or trees. A cool thing about this knot is that you can basically tighten it by hand and it will hold. You should not use it if you are putting it under a lot of strain and pressure but you can use it for tying up your tent stakes

The Timber Hitch

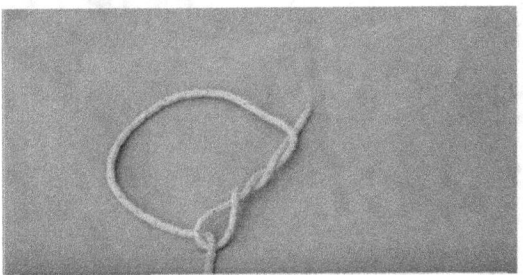

Method:

Step 1: Take one end of the rope and cross it over the other end.

Step 2: Take the tag end and wrap it around itself several times. You will get the rope looking like the one in the image below. That's all! You will notice that harder you pull on the longer end, the more secure the knot will be.

The Trucker Hitch

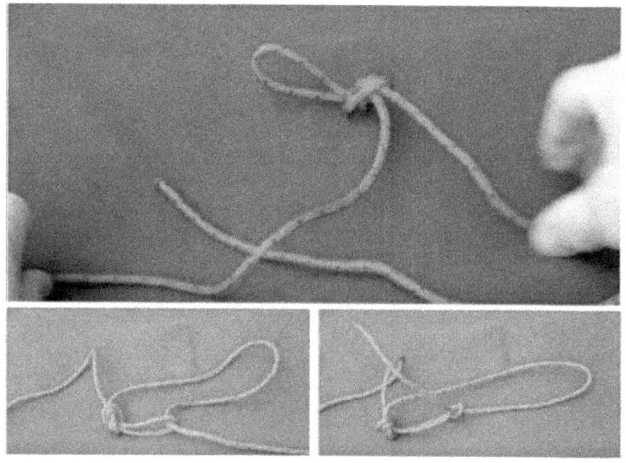

Method:

Step 1: To start with, tie an overhand knot on the main line. It's just a simple loop as in the image.

Step 2: One tag end will go around the tree or around whatever you are attaching the rope to. Then, bring the rope back through this loop you have just created.

Step 3: When you pull this end, it will tighten up, and you will be able to stretch that line really tight.

Step 4: To finish tying this knot, pinch it at the place where the long end of the rope goes through the loop and do a simple overhand knot.

<u>Cat's Paw Knot</u>

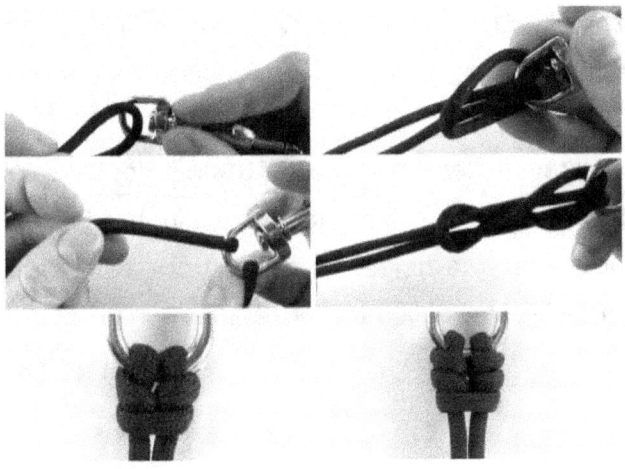

Method:

Step 1: To begin, fold a piece of cord in half and feed it through the object you are trying to attach.

Step 2: Then, pull the ends through the loop but do not tighten it.

Step 3: Spread the ends of the cord or rope and then twist the object into the knot.

Step 4: After tightening, you get a single cat's paw.

Additional steps: If you want to do a double cat's paw, repeat the same process again, but instead of turning the object once in, turn it twice, and this will give you a double cat's paw.

Truckers Hitch 2

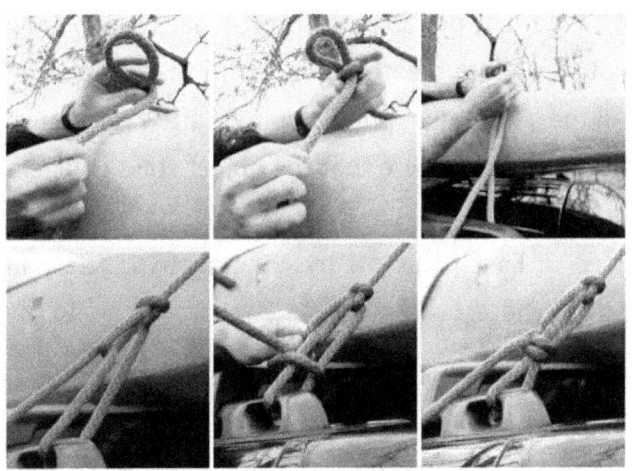

Method:

Step 1: After you wrap the object you want to secure, take the end part and twist it to make a loop.

Step 2: Take the end of the rope again and come back through the loop from the front part.

Step 3: Tighten it a bit, and you have made a loop that can easily be pulled out.

Step 4: Take the leading edge through the hook on your car, pull it back through that hole / loop you have just created, and crank that bumpy??? All the way down, pull down to tighten it as much as needed to secure that the object stays in place.

Step 5: Finish this off by creating two little half hitches here.

Taut-Line Hitch

Method:

Step 1: So, you have a rope regularly tied to, say, a tree, and then you wrap it once around another tree. Now, take the leading edge and put it over the rope and then you are going to come up and around once and then another time on the inside.

Step 2: That's twice, and then you are going to cross over, and you are going to go in the opposite direction under and through. And that's your taut-line.

Decorative Knots

Decorative knots are probably the most versatile knots you will learn how to make. You can use them for zipper pulls, bracelets, earrings, and other jewelry.

For these knots, you will mostly use paracord.

Snake Knot

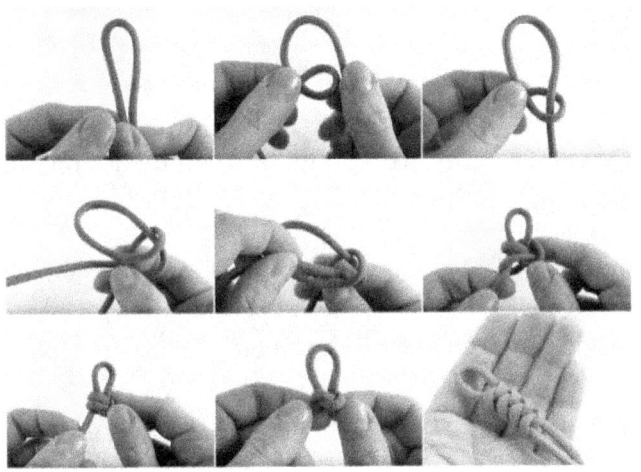

Method:

Step 1: To start, fold a piece of paracord in half.

Step 2: Make a loop on the left side, then insert the right end through this loop.

Step 3: Take the right end, place it behind the left one.

Step 4: Then, insert the end through the loop that you made.

Step 5: Tighten up the knot a bit.

Step 6: To make the second knot, flip the first knot and then place the right cord behind the left.

Step 7: Loosen up the first knot and insert the knot in through this. Then tighten it up again.

Step 8: To continue, you again should flip the knot.

Step 9: Take your right end behind the left, loosen up the knot, insert the end through and tighten it up again.

To make a series of snake knots, you will always flip the knot then insert right end through the left snake knot that you made on this side.

Cobra Knot

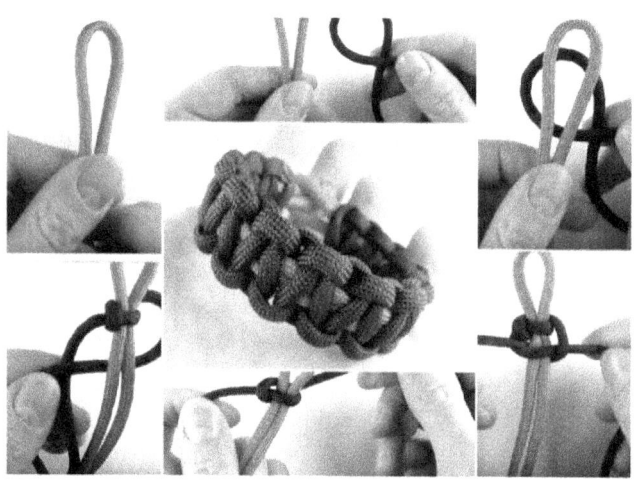

Method:

Step 1: The first thing you should do is fold a smaller piece of cord which should be about the length of your wrist plus about a foot more. Fold it in half and this is going to be the core of your bracelet.

Step 2: Take a longer piece of cord which will serve as a working cord.

Step 3: Make the basic four shape as shown in the cobra tutorial in the image above. Place it under the core.

Step 4: Pass the vertical cord over the core and through the loop.

Step 5: Tighten this and the first cobra knot is already here.

Step 6: The second cobra knot is going to be on the other side. So, the four shape is looking to the right side now. Pass the vertical cord through the loop and tighten. With this you have your first two cobra knots.

Step 7: To continue, you should alternate the sides going left and then right. You can see the pattern forming already. Continue doing this until you have enough knots to make a bracelet that fit the desired length.

Step 8: To end the bracelet, take the two ends of the cord that form the core for the bracelet.

Cross Knot

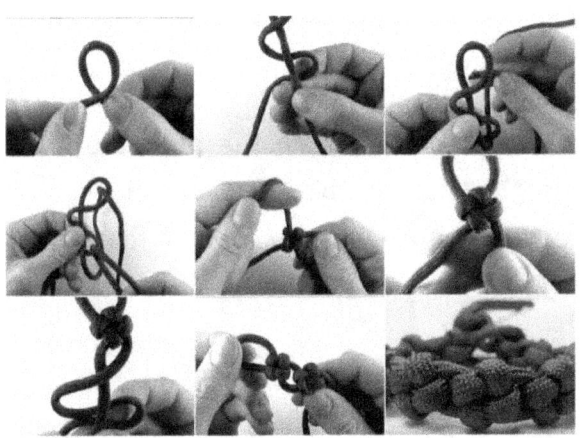

Method:

Step 1: Take a piece of paracord and make a loop.

Step 2: Pass the left cord behind the right one. This is the starting position for the cross knot.

Step 3: Take the right cord and feed the end through the back end of the top loop and then through the top of the bottom loop. This gives you the first cross knot.

Step 4: To continue, tighten it by pulling the both parts of the knot and this tightens up the knot. If the loop is a bit big, remove some of the cord by working out the knot.

Step 5: Start tying another knot the same way you did before. Pass the right cord over the left then behind two times. So, it's top down, down. Take the right cord and feed it through the back of the top loop and then through the top of the bottom loop. This knot should be next to the first knot you made. So, this requires a bit of removing of slack. The knots should be perfectly aligned to get the best look of the bracelet.

Step 6: Make more knots to get the desired length.

Cloverleaf Knot

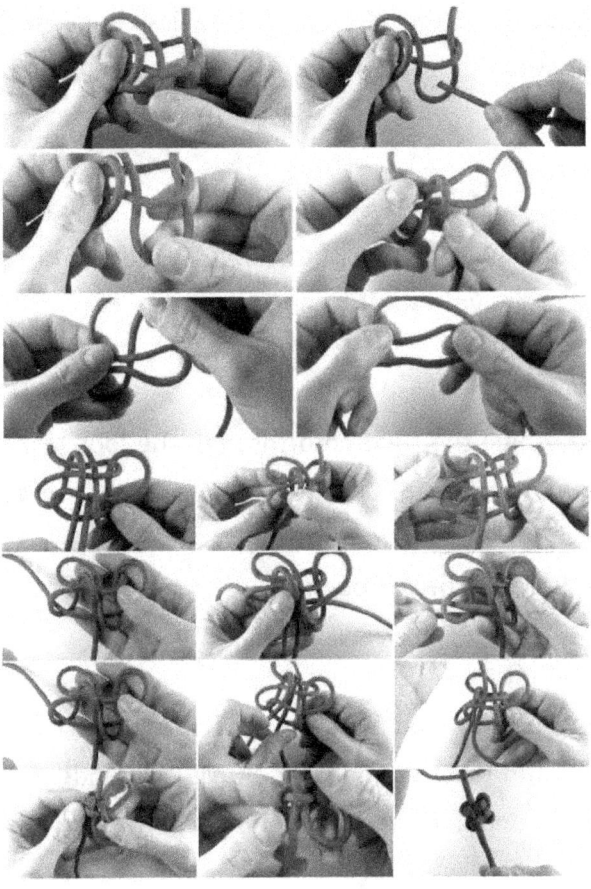

Method:

Step 1: The first thing to do is make an S shape with one piece of cord.

Step 2: Take the left end, place it behind and bring it to the front of the S shape.

Step 3: Hold this left cord in your hand, and from this point on, you will not move this left end of the cord anymore.

Step 4: Pull the right cord through the loop, take the end and feed it through the loop then over the next two cords and through the loop on the left. Pull the cord through.

Step 5: Then, you should go back under all the cords and through the loop on the right side. So, you go under three cords and then through the loop.

Step 6: Then take the end and go through the first bottom cord, then under the second two and through the top.

Step 7: With that, the knot is tied, and you should now tighten it. You tighten it by starting at one end and making your way through the knot. Remove the slack as you go. You have to tighten the knot two times to get the proper look of it.

Pipa Knot

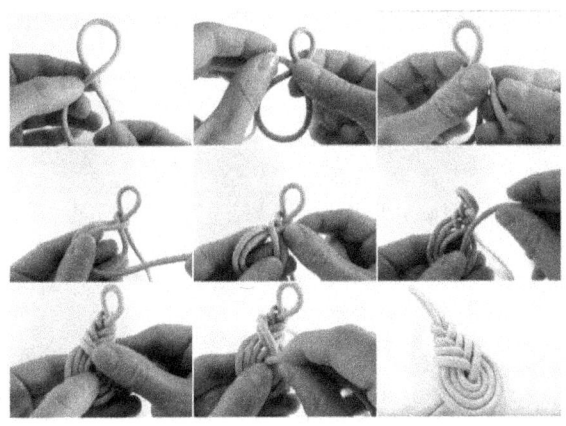

Method:

Step 1: Fold a piece of cord with the left end being smaller than the right one.

Step 2: Make a loop at the top by placing the right cord over the left.

Step 3: Make another loop at the bottom and this one will be larger.

Step 4: Then wrap around the top loop with the working end.

Step 5: Then, simply follow the first loop at the bottom on the inside.

Step 6: Then, again wrap around at the top of the loop and follow the inside loop at the bottom.

Step 7: Repeat this process until you can no longer make wraps at the bottom.

Step 8: At that point, you will take the working cord and feed it through the top of the hole at the center of the knot. By doing this the knot is tied/tight and it is tightened the usual way which is to go through the entire length of the cord and remove the slack. One thing you can do to make your tightening easier is to join the two cords at the back of the knot.

Headhunter's Knot

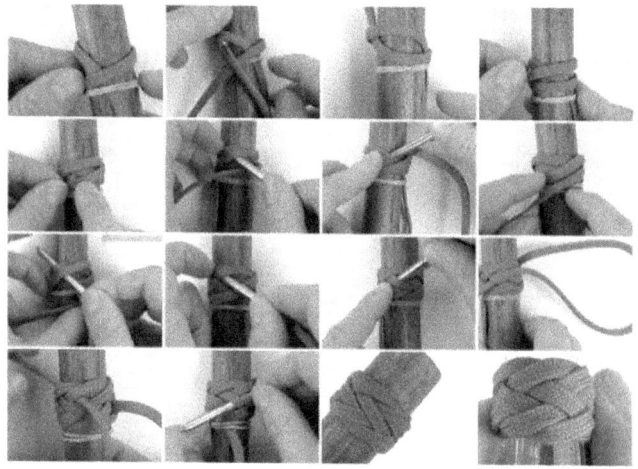

Method:

Step 1: The first thing you are going to do is form a baith around and go over the standing end.

Step 2: Then, take your working end and go under the standing end at the top.

Step 3: At the top, you are going to form another baith again by going over, and this time, you are crossing two cords, so over the standing end and over the bottom.

Step 4: You are going to form a baith at the bottom. Using your working end, you are going to go under the two.

Step 5: You are now at the top again, and this time, you have three cords. You are going to go under the first cord and over the second. You go from the top. At the bottom, you will again form a baith and enter the knot by going over and under the two.

Step 6: You are at the top again. You will enter the knot this time going under the two and over two. You are down again and you will enter the knot by going over two and under two.

Step 7: You will now have to work with five cords since you need to go over the last two. You are going to go over the first one, then under the second two and then over the last two. At the bottom, you are going to turn back up going under one, over two and under two. With this you have to come to your last pass.

Step 8: The last pass will be over two, under two and over two. With that, you have tied your headhunter's knot and now you just have to tuck in your working end with the standing ending to end it naturally. And this completes the knot.

Chapter 9: Knot Tying 101

As you learn how to work with different kinds of knots, you will encounter a lot of new words.

Without understanding what these words and phrases mean, the knot tying instructions in this book can be quite confusing.

In this chapter, we shall look at and explain the most commonly used knot tying terminologies, categories of knots, and introduce you to knot tying principles you should keep in mind:

First, let's look at an illustration of the primary sections of a knot tying model and rope.

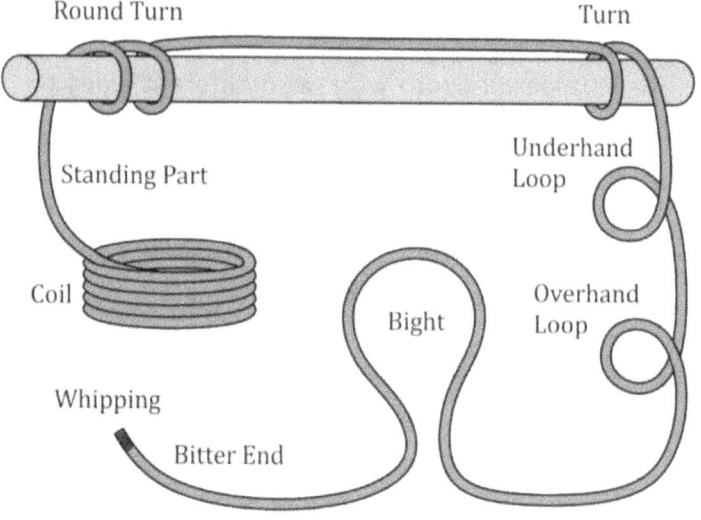

Now that the image above has given you an idea of the various parts involved in knot tying, let's discuss what each is:

Knot Tying Terminologies

The most common knot tying terminologies are:

#: Working end/whipping

Also called the running end or tag end, the working end is the free end of the rope you are working with when tying a knot.

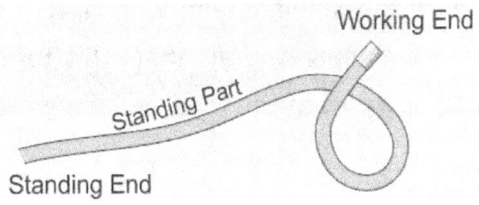

#: Standing end & standing part

The Standing end is the end of the rope that you don't manipulate when tying a knot. On the other hand, the standing part is the length of rope that faces the standing end; you also don't manipulate this part.

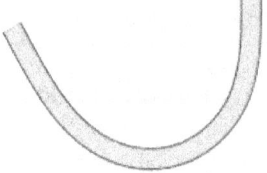

#: Bight

The bight is a sharp curve with a small radius in a rope. It's where the standing and working parts come in contact or near one another. This term can also mean any part of the rope excluding the ends.

For instance, a knot 'tied on the bight' is one where you tie the rope around the middle without manipulating any of the ends.

#: Bitter end

The bitter end is the last 1-2 inches of a rope and is often a short section with which to work.

#: Loop

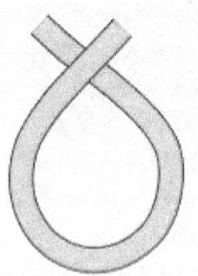

The loop is similar to a bight. The main difference between the two is that the curve has a larger radius, and the loop covers more area. This term may also refer to the part of the loop's knot or any other rope structure that encircles an object completely.

#: **Crossing point/turn**

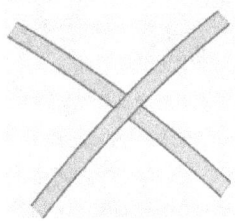

The turn is a curve where the rope crosses over itself once. For instance, if you twist a bight to 180 degrees, you end up with a crossing turn.

#: Elbow

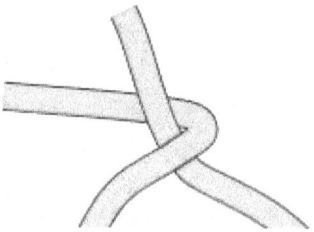

If you take the bight and twist it to an angle of 360 degrees, the elbow will be the section formed between the standing part & working end at the bottom and the crossing turn at the top.

#: Underhand and overhand

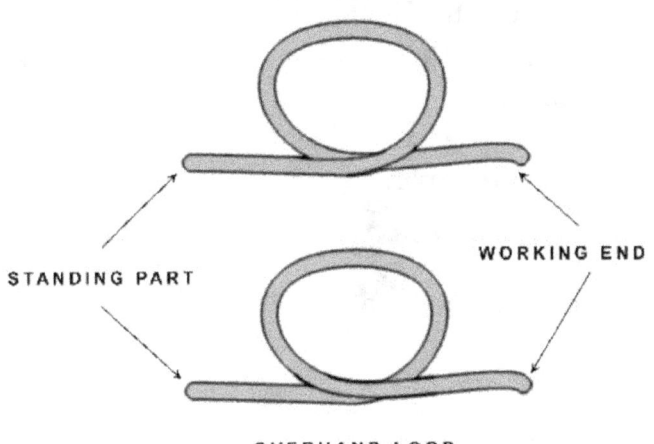

The overhand is a crossing turn where the working end loops over the standing part, while the underhand is a crossing turn where the standing part loops on top of the working part.

#: **Turn**

A turn is half a revolution of a rope around an object, such that both ends are facing the same direction, without encircling the object completely.

#: **Round turn**

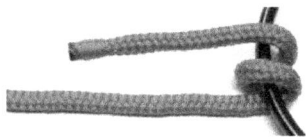

A round turn is a full revolution of a rope around a given object. The rope may wind 360 degrees around an object such that both ends face opposite directions.

The rope may also wind 540 degrees around a given object, such that both ends face the same direction. If the rope encircles the object in a couple of adjacent round turns, we call each of the revolutions a wrap.

#: **Hank**

Hank is a word used to describe lengths of rope.

Learning about knots demands that you know about the various categories of knots:

Categories Of Knots

Here are the most common categories of knots:

#: Loops

These are knots used to hold or create attachment points in a rope.

To tie it, you should tie the rope to itself to form a closed loop that you can then put around an object like a tree. These types of knot types may fit tightly or loosely around the object, and in most cases, the size is adjustable fit the object.

#: Hitches

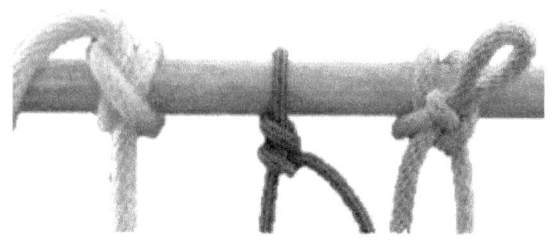

These are knots made to tie a rope onto an object at one end. As opposed to loop knots, hitches highly depend on an object for their structure; thus, they cannot exist independently.

#: Bends

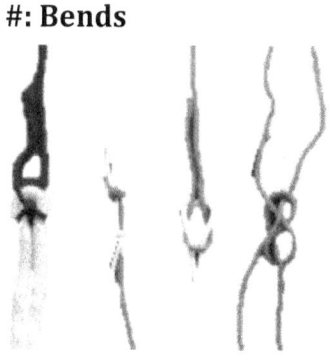

Bends are knots used to tie two different ropes together, including ropes of varying diameters

#: Lashings

These are knots used to hold two objects together. They generally work by wrapping or turning numerous rounds around two objects. These knots mostly apply to the process of building structures.

To get started with knot tying, you also need to internalize a few fundamental principles:

Knot Tying General Principles

A couple of general principles govern how we tie knots to ensure that they work efficiently.

Fundamentally, the most important thing you need to keep in mind is that when it comes to tying a perfect knot, the basic rule of thumb is to ensure that *it is easy to tie and untie and that it serves a specific purpose*.

Other principles include:

- The knot must be firm and tied tight enough such that slipping is impossible.

- The knot must be as small as possible to reduce excessive amounts of reactions when the knot comes into contact with absorbable substances.

- When tying a knot, ensure that it leaves room for no friction (sawing) in between the strands as this might weaken its integrity.

- When handling the rope, be very careful to avoid damaging it or causing weaknesses

Let's now discuss the various types of knots and their possible applications:

Chapter 10: Basic Knots

This chapter will introduce you to basic knots, show you how to tie them, and outline the advantages and disadvantages of each:

Basic Knots

Basic knots include

#: Overhand Knot

The overhand knot is one of the most common and most basic knots that most people know how to tie. It is the foundation for countless other knots and can also work as a stopper knot.

How to tie it

- Start by forming an overhand loop
- Thread the working end upward from underneath the loop

- Pull both the standing part and the working end to tighten the knot

This knot works best when applied at the end of a rope, which helps prevent it from becoming untied at the application of tension.

Advantages

Tying it is straightforward

Disadvantages

Depending on the type of rope used to tie this knot, if put under heavy loads, it can be very hard to untie, especially true if tied using very thin cordage.

Possible applications

You can use this knot can be applied when hanging a tarp. You can tie an overhand knot at the end of the rope to prevent it from sliding through the tarp's grommet.

#: The Figure 8 Knot

The figure 8 knot is another knot that you can use as a stopper knot; it's the building block for most common knots.

How to tie

- Start by forming an overhand loop
- Move the working end the standing part then around it
- Thread your working end down through the resulting loop
- Pull to tighten the knot. The result will be a knot that resembles the number 8, as illustrated above

Advantages

The figure 8 knot is very easy to tie and also easy to untie compared to the overhand knot. It is also bulkier than the overhand knot, which makes it stronger.

Disadvantages

Depending on the type of rope used to tie this knot, if it is put under heavy loads, it can be hard to untie.

Possible applications

- Since the figure-eight knot can work as a stopper knot, it can come in handy in situations where the overhand knot might slip through the hole because it is larger than the overhand knot, which makes it harder for it to slip through.

- This knot works best as a base formation for most of the complex knots used by rock climbers.

]#: Square Knot

The square knot is one of the most popular knots, mostly used to bind objects together. Some areas of the globe call it the reef knot.

Although this knot is very popular, you should use it with a lot of caution. Most people tend to use it to join two lengths of rope to create a longer rope, which is not safe because square knots tend to slip or even become untied when a load is applied.

How to tie

Hold the ends of your rope in each hand. As you do this, cross the working end in your left hand over to the one in your right hand, which will result in an 'X.'

Wrap the working end you are holding in your left hand behind then under the working end that you are holding in your right hand.

Continue wrapping the working end until it lies over the working end in your left hand—shown below

Proceed by taking the working end in your right hand then cross it over to the working end on your left hand to form another 'X.'

Wrap the working of the rope in your right hand behind then under the working end in your left hand

Continue to wrap until the working end lies over the working end in your left hand—shown below

Now you have a standing part and working end in each of your hands. Pull them away from each other to tighten the knot.

NOTE: If you tie this knot incorrectly, you will end up with a 'granny knot.' To know whether you have tied your knot correctly, check the sides.

A proper knot should have a standing part and working end over a bight. If this is not the case, then you probably tied a granny knot. Below is an instance of a square knot tied improperly.

Advantages

This knot is simple to tie and untie

Disadvantages

As mentioned earlier, this knot is not suitable for some situations, especially those that involve heavy loads. If used in such situations, it can result in injuries or even death.

When this knot is not under any tension, it can easily become untied or shake loose.

Possible applications

- You can use this knot to secure a bandage to limbs such as legs or arms.

- If you are camping and have gone out to collect some twigs for a fire, you can use this type of knot to bind your bundle together so that it's easier to carry.

- In a case where you need a makeshift belt, you can tie a length of rope around your waist and fasten it using a square knot.

#: Bowline Knot

The bowline knot is effective in cases where you might need to tie a loop at your rope's end or when you need to secure your rope around an object.

How to tie

Start by forming an overhand loop on the rope's standing part.

Move the working end of the rope upward through the resulting loop from step 1

Wrap the working end of the rope behind its standing part

Continue to move the working end into and through the overhand loop you created in step 1

Complete the knot and pull it until it is tight enough

Advantages

This knot is easy to tie and untie; it's also fairly secure. When you add load onto a rope with this knot, it tends to tighten up, not become untied, which is usually the case with most other knots.

This knot will also not constrict to the object to which you've tied it around upon application of tension to the rope's standing part.

Disadvantages

Any tension exerted on a rope with this knot makes the knot almost impossible to untie—or untying it becomes very challenging.

Possible applications

This knot has a wide range of applications. For instance, you can use it to secure the guy line of a tent. You can also use it to secure and tether a canoe or raft to a tree as it floats in water.

Chapter 11: Knots For Campers

Below are camper-friendly knots

#: Midshipman's Hitch

Almost similar to a knot called the taut-line hitch, the midshipman's hitch is a more secure option.

This knot is effective for situations where you are securing an object to an anchor point using a length of rope, and you need to adjust the tension. Once tied, this knot allows you to slide it easily along the main rope to either decrease or increase tension.

When you apply a load to the standing part of the rope, the knot stays in that position. It does not slip based on the friction generated between the rope and the knot.

How to tie

Start by passing the working end around the desired object to make a turn—shown in the image below:

Now cross your working end over the standing part of the rope

Wrap your working end around and under the ropes standing part, ensuring that the wrap is inside the loop.

Continue wrapping the working end around the first turn, ensuring that you cross over the turn and keep the second turn in the loop's part that is closest to you—shown below.

The second turn should form a crossing point over the first turn, which is responsible for creating extra friction, hence making the knot more secure.

Apply some tension to your working end to stop the knot from slipping as you complete this knot.

Continue to wrap using your working end, but this time, on the outer part of the loop. Pass your working end behind the rope's standing part—shown below

Thread your working end into the hole in the wrap you created. By doing this, you will be making a half hitch on the outer part of the loop that you formed on the standing part.

Dress the knot and pull to tighten it before applying a load. Your knot is now complete and should look like the one in the image below.

How to adjust

You can adjust this knot by grabbing it in your hand and sliding it either upwards on its standing part to make the loop bigger, or downwards to make the loop smaller.

Advantages

It is easy and quick to make adjustments to guylines with a midshipman's hitch tied onto them. Unlike other knots of similar applications, you can tie this knot when there is a load already tied on the standing part of the rope.

Disadvantages

This knot is not an ideal choice for situations where there'll be considerable amounts of tension applied to the rope. That's because the knot primarily relies on friction to prevent it from sliding, and more tension may require high amounts of friction to keep it in place. The friction generated may be insufficient to hold the tension from the load; thus, the knot will end up sliding.

The choice of material for the rope is also an important factor to consider here because slippery-type of ropes will not be able to hold their position because of a lack of sufficient friction.

Possible applications

You can use this knot to attach guylines to a tent stake, which works because after you tie the knot, you can apply tension to the guyline by sliding the knot up the standing part.

You can also use it when you want to take the tent down by sliding the knot towards the part to which you have anchored it to release the tension exerted on the guyline.

You can also use this knot to secure a rope to a tree when putting up a tarp shelter's rigid line.

You can also use it to create a makeshift clothesline.

#: Sheet Bend

Knot

Also called a weavers knot, this knot is mostly ideal in cases where you have to join two ropes that have different diameters. However, it's not limited to ropes that have varying diameters; you can also use it to join ropes with similar diameters.

How to tie

Start by making a bight on the working end of the rope with the thicker diameter. Hold it in your right hand.

Keep the 'U' of the bight facing the right and the ropes working at the bight's top.

Then take the rope with the thinner diameter and thread it upwards from the bottom of the bight you formed in step 1

Now move the working of the thin rope around and behind the bight of the other rope. It is essential to wrap it in such a way that it goes towards the direction the working end of the thick rope is facing

Thread the working end of the rope with the smaller diameter under itself—shown in the image below

Dress and then finally tighten your knot

NOTE: If you do not follow the above steps correctly, you might end up with the working ends of the two ropes on the opposite side of your knot, which will make your knot very likely to slip because of tension.

To make sure you've tied the knot correctly, make sure both working ends of the ropes are facing the top of the knot.

Advantages

Even though tying knots using ropes of different diameters can cause the knot to become unstable and prone to slipping, this knot can solve this issue.

Disadvantages

This knot tends to get loose when you apply tension on both ropes

Possible applications

If you need a longer rope, and all you have is the option of using different types of scavenged rope, all of which have different diameters, then this knot will come in handy.

#: Double Sheet Bend

The double sheet bend is a slight modification to the sheet bend knot but purposed to become more secure.

How to tie

Form a bight using the working end of the rope with the thick diameter and hold it in your left hand.

Keep the 'U' of the bight facing the right; you should position the working end at the top of the bight.

Hold the thinner rope in your right hand and thread it from the bottom of the bight going upwards.

Move the working end of the thin rope around and behind the bight. Wrap it towards the direction that the bight's working end is facing (shown in the above steps).

Thread the working end of the thin rope under itself, then create a second wrap by repeating steps 4 and 5.

Finish by tightening and dressing the knot. You will end up with a knot that looks like the one in the image below:

Possible applications

You can use this knot anywhere where you would need to use a sheet bend knot and in situations where you need a more secure knot

#: The Double Fisherman's Knot

In some situations, you may need to tie together two lengths of rope to make a longer one. This knot, in some cases referred to as the 'grapevine knot,' is what you should use in such circumstances.

This knot is a constituent of two knots that lock onto each other when you apply tension to the rope.

How to tie

Start by Laying the working ends of each of the ropes parallel to one another. Let the ends overlap by a few inches—shown in the image below. The diameter of the rope you are using will determine how much overlap you need to have. Thin ropes such as paracord will require a little overlap compared to thicker ropes that may need more overlap. As you continue to practice with this knot, you will be able to develop a sense of how much overlap you should leave.

Cross the working end of your rope over to the other ropes standing part and wrap behind it. Then move around it to the top—shown in the

image below.

Form another wrap, ensuring you keep it on the left side of the crossing point of the previous

wrap—shown below.

Thread your working end through the two wraps you formed—moving the rope below the crossing points on the two wraps.

Dress the knot and pull to tighten it. At this stage, you have completed the first part of the knot. The next part involves repeating the whole process on the other length of rope.

Cross the working end of the rope over to the other rope's standing part. When you complete this step, you should end up with the working end facing downwards—shown in the image below.

Create another wrap, ensuring you keep it at the right side of the crossing point you formed in step 6.

Thread the working end under the crossing points of both the wraps you created. Dress the knot and pull to tighten it. You have now completed the second part of the knot—which should be looking like the image below.

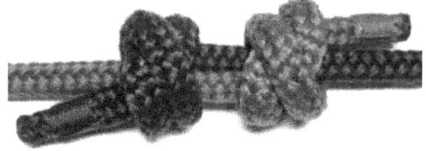

To complete the knot, pull on each of the standing parts of the two ropes. The knots will slide together, and you will end up with a knot like the one shown below.

NOTE: If you tied the knot properly, you should have a tidy and neat appearance where the two knots lie neatly against each other. When you look at the knots from the side, each of them should look like an 'X.' When you flip it, the knots should look like four diagonal lines running in parallel. The working ends from the two ropes should end up on opposite sides of the diagonals. If they are on the same side, then you have probably made a mistake, which means you will need to repeat the steps afresh.

Variation Of The Double Fisher Man's Knot

You can form an extra wrap before threading the working end under the crossing points on each knot. In this case, you will end up with the triple fisherman's knot.'

Advantages

Based on the design of this knot, it is the most effective way to tie up two lengths of rope—as it is more secure compared to other knots—to join multiple lengths of rope.

Disadvantages

When you place a heavy load on a rope with this type of knot, it can become challenging to unite it. In some cases, this knot can also be very tricky to tie.

Possible applications

In situations where you have to work with scavenged cordage, you can use this type of knot to tie together topes of multiple lengths to create one long and strong length of rope.

Chapter 12: Knots For Sailors & Fishermen

The most common sailing and fishing knots are:

#: Blood Knot

This knot is the one fishermen often use to join lines of different sizes.

How to tie

Hold the working end of the rope with the thicker diameter in your left hand and the other rope in your right hand. Cross the two lines over each other to form an 'X.' The thicker line should lie behind the thinner line.

With the index finger and thumb of your right hand, pinch the crossing point of the two lines and hold it firmly.

Wrap the working end of the thinner line around the rope with the thicker diameter in a counterclockwise direction. That means you should pass the thinner rope behind the thick one, then over the top, and finally towards you— complete at least 4-5 wraps. Once you complete the final wrap, it should be pointing downwards.

Next, pull the working end of the thinner rope towards the crossing point you made earlier, making sure that the working end of the thinner rope points upwards and lies on top of its standing part—shown in the image below.

Next, pinch the knot at the location where they meet, using your left hand to hold it in place as you continue.

Now wrap the working end of the thinner rope in a clockwise manner. That means you will have to pass the thicker line in front of the thinner rope, under it, and then finally towards you.

Make the same number of wraps you did in step 3 to make the knot symmetrical. When done, the working end should point upwards—shown below.

Now pass the working end of the thicker rope towards the working end of the thinner line. Note that the working end of the thinner rope will have to tread through the hole between the two lines pointing upwards. You should also thread the working end of the thicker rope through the same hole, though for this one, you should pass it from the top so that it points downwards.

If you correctly do this, then the working end of the thinner rope should point upwards while the working end of the thicker rope should point downwards—shown below.

The next step is to dress the knot as lightly as possible and lubricate it.

Pull the standing part of the two ropes to bring everything into place.

Once you have everything set, quickly pull the standing part again to tighten the knot. It may take a few attempts before you get it right. The appearance of the knot will change completely

Trim off the excess rope on the working ends as close to the knot as possible. The finished knot should look like the one below.

Advantages

When tied properly, this knot is very sleek and can pass through the rod guides of a fishing pole easily. The streamlined nature of this knot also helps keep it from collecting debris like water moss.

Disadvantages

This knot is not easy to learn or tie.

Note: For this knot, the blue rope represents the thicker line, while the red one represents the thinner line.

Possible applications

You can use this knot to make to create tapered leaders, which allows your fly-fishing line to roll out smoothly and settle on the water gently without making a splash.

#: Surgeon's Knot

The surgeon's knot is another useful fishing knot, mainly used to join two lengths of line. However, unlike the blood knot, this one only works with two lines that have an almost exact or similar diameter. Drastically differing diameters will not work with this knot.

How to tie

Start by laying the main fishing line and the new section you are tying in parallel to each other. Have the working end of both ropes overlap each other by a few inches. The two lines should also be pointing in the same direction.

Form the overlapped sections of both ropes into an overhand loop.

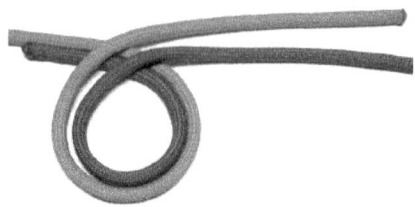

Pass the working ends of the two lines through the loop you created to form a simple overhand knot.

Now repeat the previous step so that you can have a knot that appears like the one shown below.

Lubricate it and then pull to tighten it. To complete the knot, just trim off the working ends as close as possible to the knot

Advantages

This knot is very strong and extremely simple to tie. It also does not weaken the line—as is the case with other knots

Disadvantages

This knot is not suitable for tying a long extension onto your reel because you cannot easily tie it in the middle of the line.

The knot is also larger in diameter than the blood knot; thus, it might cause jams in some fishing rods.

NOTE: The red rope represents the longer fishing line connected to your reel. The blue rope represents the shorter section of the tippet or leader supposed to tie onto the end of your mainline.

Possible applications

You can use this knot to tie a leader onto your fishing line or to tie tippets at the end of fly-fishing leaders.

#: Palomar Knot

Being one of the knots used most used by fishermen, here's how to tie the Palomar knot:

How to tie

Start by threading the working end of your line into the eyelet of your lure or hook.

Then pass your working end back through the hook's eyelet —as shown below. You will end up with a bight going through the eyelet.

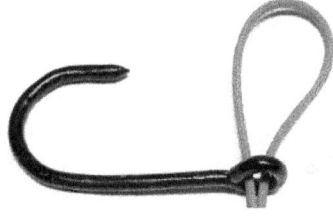

Next, cross your bight over both the standing part and working end of your line—shown below.

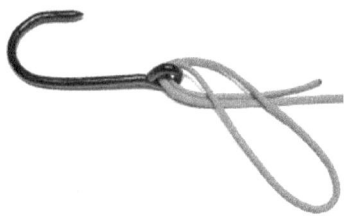

Now tie a loose overhand knot using the bight as you take care not to twist it. However, do not tighten the knot all the way at this level. Leave it a bit loose.

Pass the bight over the lure or hook—shown below.

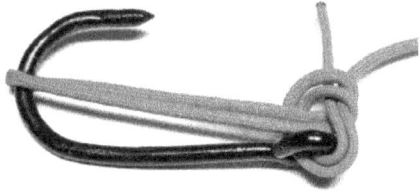

Next, move your bight gently towards the standing end of your line. Ensure you pass your bight over and around the overhand you created in step 4.

Then pull the standing part and the working end slowly to allow the knot to tighten. Before the knot tightens all the way, lubricate it.

Hold the lure or hook carefully as you pull the standing part and the working end to fully tighten the knot.

Snip off the working end as close to the knot as possible. Your Palomar knot is now complete.

Advantages

This knot is compatible with most fishing lines and does not slip as much as other knots.

Most of the fishing lines available in the market today have different features that affect their ability to hold knots without slipping. The Palomar knot is ideal as it can hold a knot without slipping, whether you are using the latest fishing lines or typical monofilament fishing lines.

Disadvantages

If tied incorrectly, then it might not work well with some types of fishing lines, thus causing your line to have higher chances of breaking at the knot.

Possible applications

This knot's main use is to tie a lure or hook onto a fishing line

#: The Figure 8 Loop

If you want a knot that is more secure than the figure 8 knot, you can consider going for the figure 8 loop, which is commonly used by rock climbers and mountaineers.

How to tie

Start by forming a bight in the position where you want to tie your figure 8 loop.

Next, form an underhand loop on the bight.

Now move the bight's head over the standing part and the working end then around the two.

Continue to move it through the loop, and then dress the resulting knot by flipping the part near the loop. Pull it hard to tighten it

Advantages

The figure 8 loop knot is easy to tie at any position, even the middle of the rope, as long as there is no tension applied.

Disadvantages

Depending on the type of rope used, you might struggle to untie this knot if there is a considerable amount of tension applied to the rope.

Possible applications

You can use this knot by attaching an object to it's working end or to a section of the rope's standing part. You can also create a loop on the standing part, which you can then use to tie another rope onto, which can come in handy in various situations such as securing loads to a boat or a trailer.

#: Two Half Hitch

Also called the double half hitch, you can tie this knot is simply by tying two half hitch knots. A half hitch knot is an overhand hand knot tied onto an object. It is a kind of binding knot used to attach cordage onto objects like trees. Tying two ½ hitch knots makes it more secure.

How to tie

Hold the working end of the rope in your hand and pass it around an object of your choice, which will form a single turn.

Next, pass the working end to the front of the rope's standing part—shown in the image below.

Thread the working of the rope through the loop you created in the previous step and pull to tighten, which will be your first half hitch.

Now pass the working end of the rope around its standing part again. However, this time, keep the wrap outside of the loop.

Now form the second half hitch by threading the working end into the second loop.

Then dress the knot before pulling both the half

hitches to tighten.

Advantages

When you apply pressure to its standing part, this basic binding knot tends to hug the object you've tied it onto tightly. That fact makes it effective in situations where you do not want the knot moving from its original position when you tie it.

Disadvantages

In cases where you don't want a knot that constricts, such as when tying an animal, you cannot use this knot.

Possible applications

When hanging a hammock, you can use this knot to attach the ends of the ropes to two trees. Since this knot will constrict around the tree, the friction produced between the bark of the tree and the rope will prevent the rope from sliding down once you lie on the hammock.

If you are constructing a simple tarp shelter, you can use this knot to attach a rope's end to the tarp's grommet.

When camping, you can use the 2-half hitch to attach a tent's guy-lines to the rainfly.

#: Two-Half Hitch With A Bight

Being a handy variation to the two-half hitch described above, here's how to tie this knot:

How to tie

Hold the working end in your hand and then pass it around the object of your choice, like a pole or tree. The result will be a single turn.

Now proceed to pass the working end of the rope in front of its standing part.

Then thread the working end into the loop you created. Pull it to tighten.

Use the remaining part of your working end to form a bight. This step makes it easy to untie the knot. Pass it around the standing part, but ensure you keep the war outside the loop.

Then form the second half of the hitch by threading the bight through the loop you created.

Dress your knot, then pull both the half hitches to tighten.

Advantages

Although this knot is almost similar to the 2-half hitch, it is both easy and quick to untie and tie.

Disadvantages

Because this knot is easy to tie and untie, it could become loose, even in situations when you don't want it to be so. That, therefore, means it is less secure than the 2-half hitch.

Possible applications

You can use this knot for similar purposes as the 2 half-hitch knots. However, this specific variation can be useful in situations where you need to untie something quickly later. All you have to do is grab hold of the working end and pull it, which will, in turn, force the night to pull through the send ½ hitch, hence untying it.

#: The Round Turn And The 2-Half Hitch Knot

As another variation of the 2-half hitch knot, here's how to tie this knot:

How to tie

Start by passing your rope around an object to form a complete round turn as shown below

Now pass the working end of the rope in front of its standing part—shown below.

Then thread the working end into the loop formed in the previous step. Pull to tighten, which will form the first half of the hitch.

Now pass your working end around the standing part of the rope again, but this time, keep the wrap outside the loop.

Now thread the working end into the second loop you created above to form the second half hitch.

Dress the knot, then proceed to pull on the two half-hitches to tighten. Your knot is now complete and should look like the one shown below

Advantages

This variation offers more friction on the object onto which you've tied it. It, therefore, drastically reduces slipping by spreading the load's weight on the rope on two turns as opposed to one, which makes the knot stronger, thus less likely to break.

Disadvantages

Tying this knot takes longer than the two-half hitch, but the added strength makes up for this time.

Possible applications

You can use this knot in situations where you need to secure a rope to stationary objects. You can also use it in most situations where you use the two-half hitch, but with the added advantage of more surface area on an object, thus making the knot much stronger

As an example, you can use this knot to tie a boat to a cleat.

Chapter 13: Knots For Rock Climbers & Mountaineers

Below are knots ideal for mountaineers and rock climbers:

#: Figure 8 Follow-Through Knot

This knot is a variation of the figure 8 loop knot, but a bit more complex and secure.

How to tie

Start by tying a figure 8 knot on the working end of your rope. Ensure you leave at least a few inches of extra rope so that you can complete the 'follow-through' section of the knot. As you continue to practice, you will start getting a sense of how much rope you need to leave.

Pass your working end around—and through—the item you'd like the loop to encompass——shown below.

Loosen the figure 8 knot you made in step 1 to enlarge it slightly, an important step that will help you finish the remaining steps easily.

Now thread the working end through the spaces you created when you enlarged your figure-eight knot. The aim here is to retrace it, which means you should be precise as you do this. The image below shows you how your knot should look like after this step.

Now dress the knot by flipping the top strand of the rope near the standing part downwards. Your knot should look symmetrical when you look at it from both sides of the knot and both ends of the '8.'

Pull the knot to tighten it. Your knot is now complete

Optional steps

As an added measure of security and safety, you can tie a backup knot to the standing part of your rope using the extra portion of the working end. How to tie

Hold both the working end and the standing part above the knot. Now cross your working end over the standing part—shown below.

Wrap the working end around and behind to the front. That will result in a wrap around your standing part. You will have formed a crossing point now.

Keep the crossing point between the figure 8 and the crossing point as shown below.

Now thread your working end through the two wraps. Ensure to pass it below the crossing points and away from the figure 8 knot—shown below.

Then pull on the working end of your rope to tighten and backup the knot. If you tie it correctly, it should look like an '=' on one side and an 'X' on the other side.

NOTE: This knot is intricate and used in very critical applications. After you tie it, you should inspect the knot thoroughly to ensure that you tied it correctly. You can even have someone double-check it for you.

Advantages

You can rely on this knot for more critical applications and when you want a more robust knot.

Disadvantages

This knot takes more time to tie than simpler knots such as the bowline. Additionally, you should take special attention to ensure you tie and dress this knot, especially if you are going to use it in critical applications.

Possible applications

This knot can be ideal in rock climbing and mountaineering based on how secure it is. However, you should get training from a qualified instructor before using it. You should also practice a lot before you apply it in a real-life situation.

#: One-Handed Bowline Knot

There are many variations to the bowline knot. The one-handed bowline knot can come in handy in a case where you need to tie a bowline around the waist. To tie this knot, you should only use one hand—preferably your prominent hand.

How to tie

Start by holding the working end of your rope and passing it around your waist. Pass it in a way that ensures the working end is on the right side of your body, and the standing part of the rope is on the left side of your body.

Now ensure you hold the working end with your right hand. Leave about 7-8 inches of rope between the position you are holding and the end of the rope.

Cross the working end—still in your right hand—over the standing part of the rope on the left side of your body

With a twisting motion, bend your right wrist and move the working end over the standing part, then towards your belly button—shown below.

Using your thumb, hook the standing part of the rope.

Now slightly twist the rope in your right hand until you eventually end up with an overhand loop wrapped around your hand—shown below. The working end should be on the right side of the standing part.

Using your index finger, pass the working end of the rope behind the standing part.

Hook the working end using your thumb and bring it around the standing part.

Grab the working end and pull it to go through the loop that is now encircling your hand.

Now pull the knot as tightly as possible to complete your one-handed bowline.

Possible applications

Besides rock climbing and mountaineering, you can also use this knot in many other situations where you can only use one hand to make a knot.

You need to practice creating this knot until it becomes as easy as tying your shoelaces because, during an emergency, you will have to be very fast, and you will have to rely on your instincts and memory to tie the knot.

#: One-Handed Bowline For Fishing

Picture this:

You've gone fishing, and your boat/canoe capsizes., but you manage to hold onto something. Someone throws you a rope to rescue you, but you need to keep holding onto the object as you tie the rope around your waist.

In such a case, if you know how to tie the one-handed bowline, you can tie the rope around your waist quickly with one hand so that the person can pull you to the shore and safety.

#: Autoblock Knot

The autoblock knot is an easy-and-quick to tie friction knot mostly used as a backup for grapples. This knot is usually made using either temporary or factory-made loops to griping any direction and can be slid freely over a rope during a time of controlled descent.

How to tie

Wrap your autoblock cord around four to five times around your rappel ropes. Ensure you use a thin cord to do this—like the 5mm or the 6mm static cordage. Use most of the length of the cord on wrapping because the more wraps you make, the more friction generated.

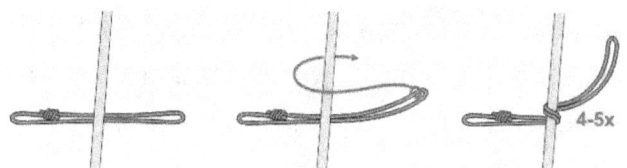

Clip both ends of your cord into your harness leg loop's locking carabiner. Lock the carabiner so that your cord doesn't become undone. Lastly, you should arrange all the wraps until they look neat – not crossing each other.

#: Valdotain Tresse knot

Also called the VT knot, the use of this friction knot is common when descending and ascending on ropes. It is most popular with arborists.

How to tie

Make at least 4 wraps around the main rope using a sewn prusik, spliced eye split tail, or hand-tied friction cord as shown in the image below

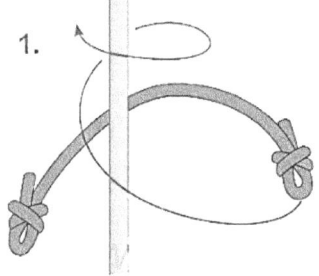

1.

After doing the fourth wrap, bring the two ends down on the same level

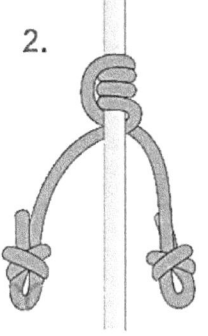

2.

Now cross the two lines in front of the main rope then cross them again at the back. That will add up to a total of 6 wraps

3.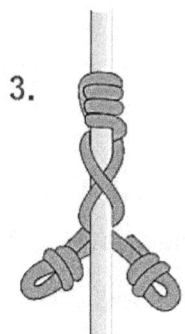

Join the eyes of your rope in front of the main rope and clip them together using a carabiner

4.

#: Munter Hitch

This knot provides a method for rappelling and belaying without using a rappel/belay device. This knot works best with a large and pear-shaped carabiner, and you should only use it with a locking carabiner.

When belaying using this knot, you should ensure that the rope you are using to carry the load is next to the carabiner's spine. It is vital to set up this knot correctly before use because if set incorrectly, it may be life-threatening to the person at the end of this rope.

How to tie

Make a loop on your rope, then slip it into a locking carabiner. Create another loop with the part of the rope crossing opposite the loop you made first.

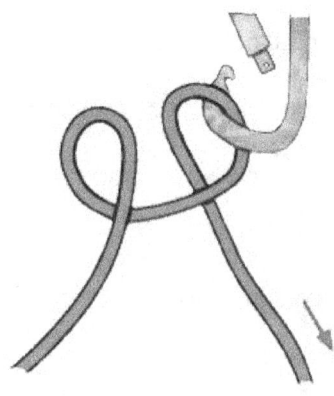

Now Slip the second loop you made into your carabiner and lock it

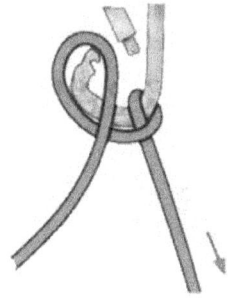

Ensure the strand of rope that carries the load is next to the spine of your carabiner—the strand with the red arrow below. Never put a load of the strand near the mechanism.

Chapter 14: Knots For Farms & Animals

The following knots are ideal for farm animals and farming-related applications:

#: Prusik Knot

Also called the prusik hitch, this knot can come in handy in situations where you want to attach an object on the standing part of a given length of rope. For this knot to work effectively, you should use a thinner rope than the main rope used.

How to tie

Start by deciding the size you want your loop to be, which will mostly depend on the number of times you'd like to wrap your loop around the main rope. The more wraps you will need, the larger the loop you will have to create.

Now cut a length of rope, leaving a few extra inches longer than the overall circumference you would like your loop to have.

Tie the ends of the rope you cut using the double fisherman's knot, as illustrated in the image below;

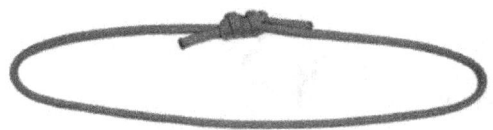

Then lay the loop you created above behind the main rope as shown below

Move the end of the loop that has the fisherman's knot around and over the main rope. The knot should pass through the loop, which results in a complete wrap around the main rope as shown in the image below

Repeat threading the end of the loop—as illustrated in the step above—for at least three more times. However, be very careful as you do this, and ensure that every wrap you make does not cross over the previous one.

Having created the wraps around the main rope, double-check to see if they are lying neatly and not crossing over each other.

If they are okay, you can now proceed to apply tension to the end of the loop with the fisherman's knot. If some wraps do not look like they are snuggling up around the main rope tightly, you should try and manipulate them with your fingers.

NOTE: If you have tied this knot correctly, and you apply enough tension to the rope, then you should not be able to move the position of the knot along the main rope.

Advantages

You can easily attach this knot to a rope that already has tension applied to it. It is also useful because when you apply tension or a load to it, the friction produced hinders it from sliding on the main rope.

Another advantage is that when you remove tension, the knot can easily slide to another position along the main rope.

Conclusion

So from all the numerous knot tying projects that we tackled I hope that you learned a lot from it and I am glad that you now have the fundamentals of the different knot tying methods that you can do in the comforts of your own home.

Once you mastered the techniques rest assured that you can do any knot tying projects of your choice in the future. The projects that we tackled are your stepping stone for you to learn and improve. You can do those projects and other projects that you wish to do with knots on your past time.

Also, if you already think that your works are already excellent you can consider selling them for you to earn some money. Knot tying is in demand nowadays because of their stylish look.

The good thing with knots is that they are considered as multipurpose and you can use it to create different accessories that you can wear t0 add up some wow factor to your current outfit.

Knot tying is also a great way to help you to surpass crisis situations because they are very useful and can be a way to save lives such as if someone is drowning or there is a need to climb very tall places that do not give you an access to stairs then this is a great way to reach it just like when there is a fire in the area.

www.ingramcontent.com/pod-product-compliance
Lightning Source LLC
Chambersburg PA
CBHW050405120526
44590CB00015B/1831